EXTREMELY Weird ANIMALS

PLATYPUS

BY CHRISTINA LEAF

BELLWETHER MEDIA • MINNEAPOLIS, MN

Jump into the cockpit and take flight with Pilot books. Your journey will take you on high-energy adventures as you learn about all that is wild, weird, fascinating, and fun!

This edition first published in 2014 by Bellwether Media, Inc.

No part of this publication may be reproduced in whole or in part without written permission of the publisher. For information regarding permission, write to Bellwether Media, Inc. Attention: Permissions Department, 5357 Penn Avenue South, Minneapolis, MN 55419.

Library of Congress Cataloging-in-Publication Data

Leaf, Christina, author.
  Platypus / by Christina Leaf.
    pages cm. – (Pilot. Extremely Weird Animals)
  Summary: "Engaging images accompany information about platypuses. The combination of high-interest subject matter and narrative text is intended for students in grades 3 through 7."– Provided by publisher.
  Audience: Ages 7-12.
  Includes bibliographical references and index.
  ISBN 978-1-62617-076-6 (hardcover : alk. paper)
  1. Platypus–Juvenile literature. I. Title.
  QL737.M72L43 2014
  599.2'9–dc23
                            2013037772

Printed in the United States of America, North Mankato, MN.

TABLE OF CONTENTS

ON THE HUNT

A platypus waddles across the grass in the Australian twilight. Then it glides over rocks and splashes into a shallow, fast-flowing stream. Under the water, it shakes its head back and forth rapidly. This motion helps the platypus search for food in the water.

The platypus swims low. It brushes over many rocks at the bottom of the stream. It ducks its bill under the leaves and sticks that line the stream floor. To propel itself forward, the platypus paddles with its large front flippers.

Suddenly, the platypus senses a tasty worm with its bill. It dives to the floor of the stream. It disappears in a cloud of sand as it digs for the worm with its bill. When it emerges from the water, the platypus has the worm in its mouth. The hunt was a success and now it's time to eat!

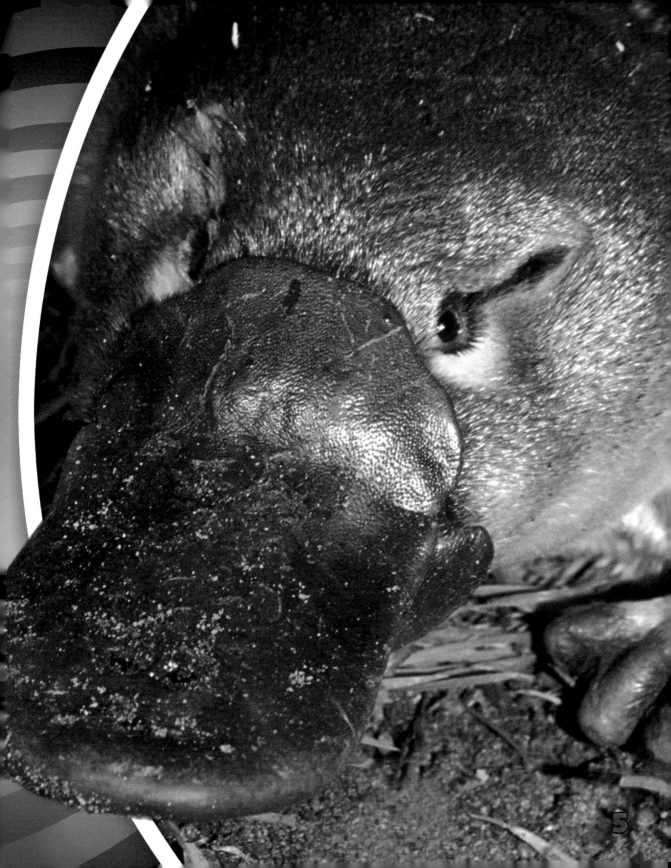

5

SEMIAQUATIC MAMMAL

The platypus is a small, furry mammal. Its head and body usually grow to be around 15 inches (38 centimeters) long, and it weighs about 3 pounds (1.4 kilograms). This strange-looking creature is often described as a mixture of three different animals. Its body looks like an otter's because it has a thick coat of brown fur. The platypus's tail is around 5 inches (13 centimeters) long. It is wide and flat like a beaver's tail. A large bill and webbed feet are the duck-like features of the platypus.

Platypuses are stocky animals. They have short legs and broad shoulders. This gives them a slight waddle when they walk. Their body shape and way of walking is similar to many reptiles. When platypuses run, the webbing on their feet retracts to expose their nails. These claws dig into the ground to make running easier.

human

platypus

Platypuses are found on the eastern coast of Australia and a few nearby islands. Environments here range from hot, wet lowlands to cool, high altitudes. Platypuses build burrows by rivers and streams. They also make their homes near lakes and ponds. Most of the time, platypuses live alone. However, several of them may live around the same body of water.

platypus range = ⬜

Always Hungry

A platypus spends 12 hours a day searching for food! It stores food in its cheek pouches when underwater.

Platypuses live close to water because they are semiaquatic animals. They spend much of their time in the water searching for food. They hunt for insects, worms, shellfish, and other small animals at the bottom of rivers and streams. When they are not swimming, they return to their burrow on land.

Toothless

Adult platypuses don't have teeth. Instead they have rough pads in their mouth to help them grind down food. They also use gravel to help with grinding.

Platypuses are uniquely adapted for a life in the water. Webbed feet help the platypus swim smoothly. The webbing pushes the water so it can move farther and faster. A platypus's hind feet and tail steer while its front feet paddle. Its thick coat is waterproof, which keeps it warm while swimming.

Folds of skin protect a platypus's eyes and ears from water during long dives. Its nostrils also close up. This means the platypus has limited senses when hunting. In order to find food underwater, the platypus uses its soft, flexible bill. This super sensitive feature can feel other living creatures in the water using electrolocation.

Animal muscles give off small electric fields that change when the muscles move. Scientists believe that the platypus's bill uses these fields to sense how far away an animal is. The platypus waves its head back and forth to find where this electrical signal is strongest. Once the platypus locates the best signal, it digs in the bottom until it finds a meal.

LAYING EGGS

Platypuses are unusual for more reasons than their strange appearance. Almost all mammals give birth to live young. Platypuses do not. They belong to a special group of mammals called monotremes, which lay eggs instead of giving birth. Platypuses and echidnas are the only two monotremes in the world.

Female platypuses lay between one and three eggs at a time. Most lay two eggs. A female builds a nest inside her burrow for the eggs. First, she uses her sharp claws and powerful legs to dig deeper into the burrow. Next, she gathers wet sticks and leaves. A damp nest keeps the eggs and babies from getting too dry. Right before laying her eggs, the female plugs the entrance so predators and high water cannot get in.

echidna

Dig Deep!
A female will sometimes dig a tunnel 100 feet (30 meters) long for her eggs.

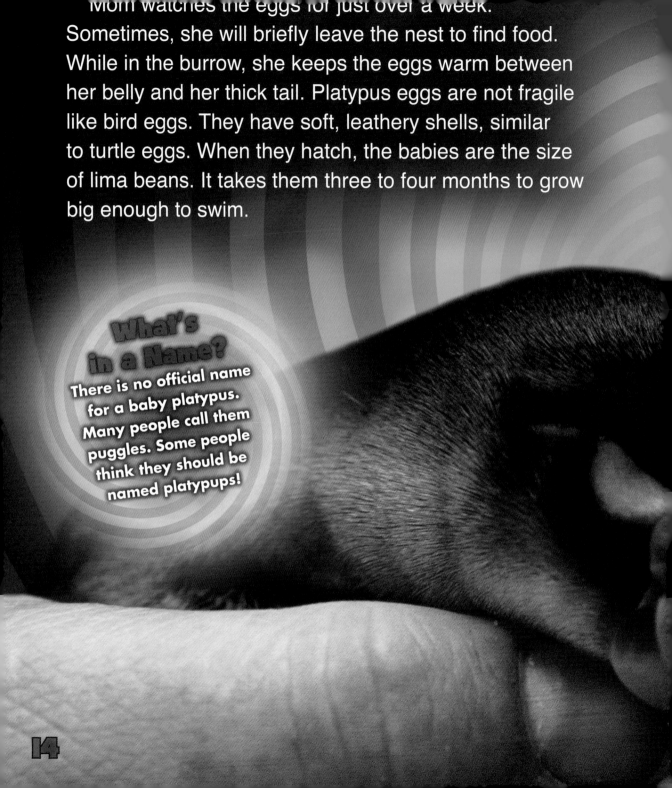

Mom watches the eggs for just over a week. Sometimes, she will briefly leave the nest to find food. While in the burrow, she keeps the eggs warm between her belly and her thick tail. Platypus eggs are not fragile like bird eggs. They have soft, leathery shells, similar to turtle eggs. When they hatch, the babies are the size of lima beans. It takes them three to four months to grow big enough to swim.

What's in a Name?

There is no official name for a baby platypus. Many people call them puggles. Some people think they should be named platypups!

While the babies are growing, the female makes milk for them. Most mammals have teats that babies suck on to get milk. Monotremes do not. A female platypus oozes milk from glands on each side of her belly. Then the babies suck up the milk for food.

DANGEROUS CREATURE

Male platypuses have small spurs on their hind legs. They look like claws that stick out of their heels. These spurs are full of venom. Platypuses are one of the few venomous mammals in the world.

venom gland

Scientists do not fully understand the purpose of these spurs. Animals often develop unique features to help them stay safe from predators or find food. The male platypus's spurs can harm enemies, but scientists believe that is not their main purpose. Male platypuses only produce their venom during mating season. This makes scientists think the spurs are for fighting off other males or protecting females.

Platypus venom is hard to study. Since females do not have spurs, scientists can only study males. The fact that the venom is only produced during a small part of the year also makes research difficult. Scientists have trouble getting samples to examine. From what has been discovered, they do know that platypus venom has several unique toxins. These are not found in any other animal. Scientists are still learning all the effects these newly discovered toxins can have.

Scientists estimate that there are more than 80 different toxins in platypus venom. Many of those are also found in the venom of lizards, snakes, and spiders. By comparing different venoms, scientists know that platypus venom is strong. It would be enough to kill a small dog. Though it is not powerful enough to kill a human, it would cause a lot of pain.

spur

I've Got a Feeling
Painkillers offer no relief for people who have experienced the platypus's spur. Only numbing the area can take away the pain.

PROTECTED BY LAW

Platypuses are fairly common animals and are of least concern. Australia already has laws to protect them. The platypus's biggest threat is habitat loss. Dry weather has made streams and rivers dry up. Sometimes people drain the water for use on farms or in their houses. This also causes river levels to drop.

Climate change from human activity affects the platypus's habitats in a different way. It makes tropical storms stronger so they have more rainfall and forceful winds. This can cause platypus' burrows to flood, which kills many adults and babies. Platypuses also face poor water quality near cities. This comes from pollution. Though platypuses are not yet in danger, humans have to be careful to protect these marvelously weird creatures.

| EXTINCT |
| EXTINCT IN THE WILD |
| CRITICALLY ENDANGERED |
| ENDANGERED |
| VULNERABLE |
| NEAR THREATENED |
| LEAST CONCERN |

Platypus Fact File

Common Name: platypus

Scientific Name: Ornithorhynchus anatinus

Famous Features: duck-like bill, webbed feet, flat tail, venom spurs; lays eggs

Distribution: east coast of Australia, Tasmania

Habitats: streams and other bodies of freshwater

Diet: insects, worms, shellfish, other bottom-dwelling animals

Life Span: up to 13 years in the wild

Current Status: least concern

GLOSSARY

altitudes—the heights of something above sea level

burrows—holes in the ground made by animals for shelter or protection

climate change—a long-lasting change in weather patterns; climate change is often traced to burning fossil fuels like oil and coal.

electric fields—areas of energy around electrically-charged things

electrolocation—an animal's ability to locate other animals by sensing a change in their electric fields

mammal—an animal that has a backbone, hair, and feeds its young milk

pollution—harmful substances that affect an environment

reptiles—cold-blooded animals with scaly skin such as snakes, lizards, and turtles

retracts—draws back or takes in

semiaquatic—living near and often entering water

spurs—stiff, sharp, pointed parts on the heels of male platypuses

stocky—short, sturdy, and thick in build

teats—small bumps most female mammals have through which babies drink milk

toxins—poisonous substances made naturally by living creatures

tropical storms—powerful storms with strong winds that begin over warm ocean waters

venom—a poison produced by some animals to harm or kill prey

webbed feet—feet with thin skin that connects the toes

TO LEARN MORE

AT THE LIBRARY

Kras, Sara Louise. *Platypuses*. Mankato, Minn.: Capstone Press, 2010.

Lunis, Natalie. *Electric Animals*. New York, N.Y.: Bearport Pub., 2011.

Myers, Jack. *The Puzzle of the Platypus: And Other Explorations of Science in Action*. Honesdale, Penn.: Boyds Mills Press, 2008.

ON THE WEB

Learning more about platypuses is as easy as 1, 2, 3.

1. Go to www.factsurfer.com.

2. Enter "platypuses" into the search box.

3. Click the "Surf" button and you will see a list of related Web sites.

With factsurfer.com, finding more information is just a click away.

INDEX